Published by
Kevredna Limited
PO Box 761
Truro
Cornwall TR1 9JE
United Kingdom
evocativecornwall.co.uk

Printed by
TJ Books
Trecerus Industrial Estate
Padstow
Cornwall PL28 8RW
tjbooks.co.uk

Graphic Design by
Niamh McClymont
nymcreative.com

ISBN 978-0-9955793-5-4

kevredna
the Cornish verb 'to share'
We donate 10% of our annual
profit to Cornish charities.

All images © Kevredna Limited
All rights reserved

Evocative Cornwall
Address Book
with perpetual calendar

evocative cornwall®

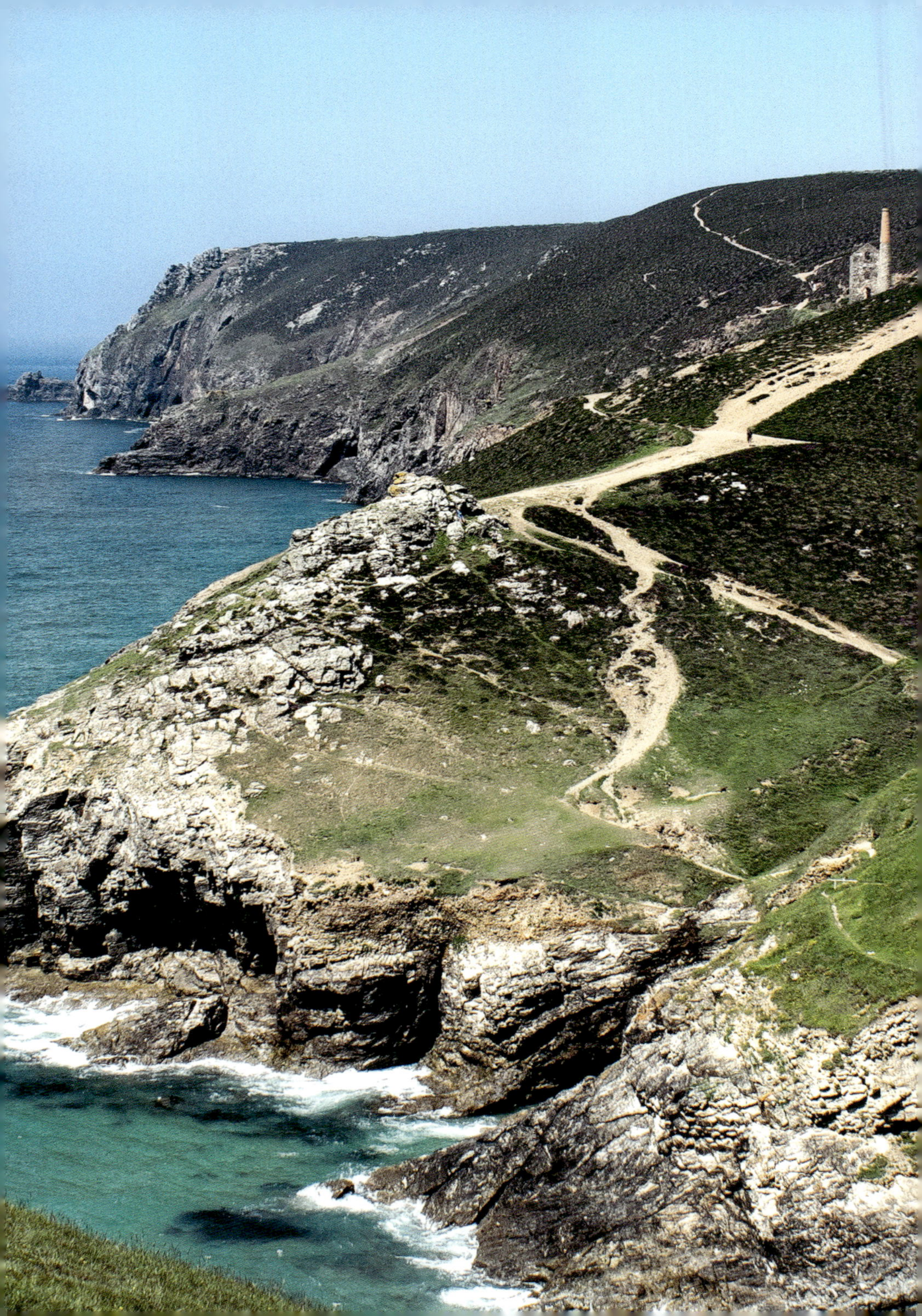

A

name & address phone

email

email

email

email

email

email

email

towards St Agnes Head

A

name & address **phone**

email

email

email

email

email

email

email

A

name & address　　　　　　　　　　　**phone**

email

email

email

email

email

email

email

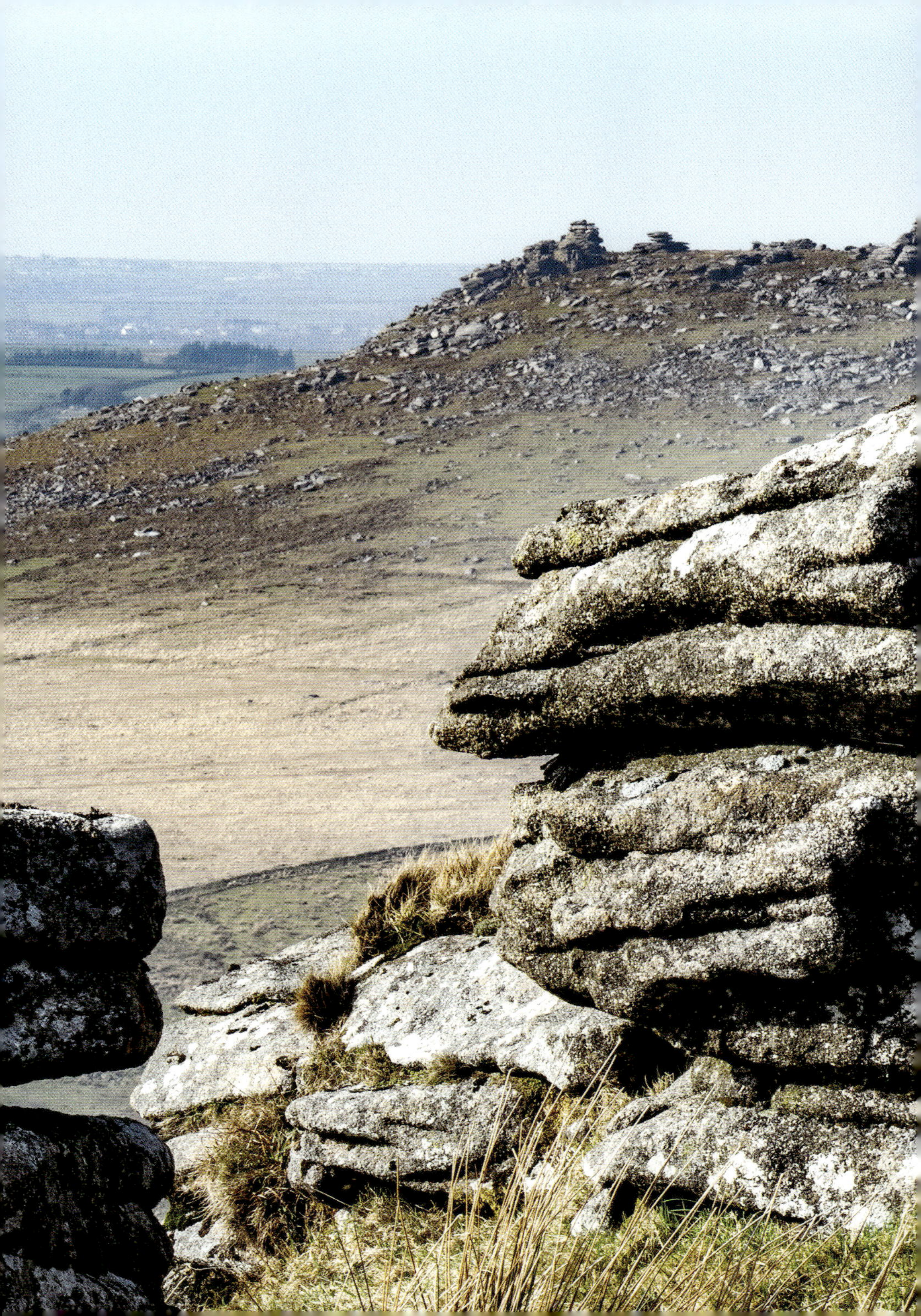

B

name & address　　　　　　　　　　**phone**

email

email

email

email

email

email

email

Bodmin Moor

B

name & address **phone**

email

email

email

email

email

email

email

B

name & address **phone**

email

email

email

email

email

email

email

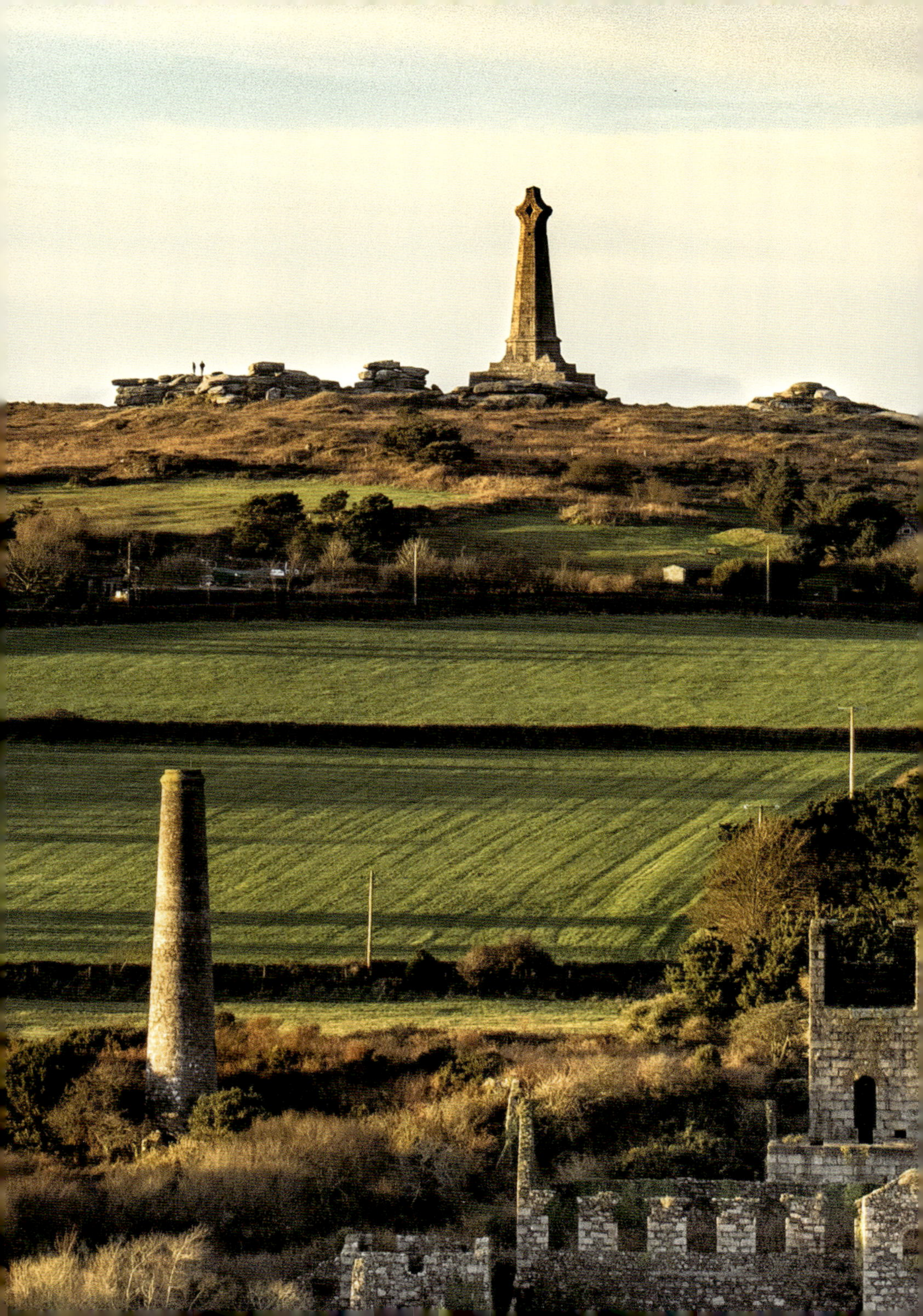

C

name & address **phone**

email

email

email

email

email

email

email

Carn Brea

C

name & address phone

email

email

email

email

email

email

email

C

name & address　　　　　　　　　　　**phone**

email

email

email

email

email

email

email

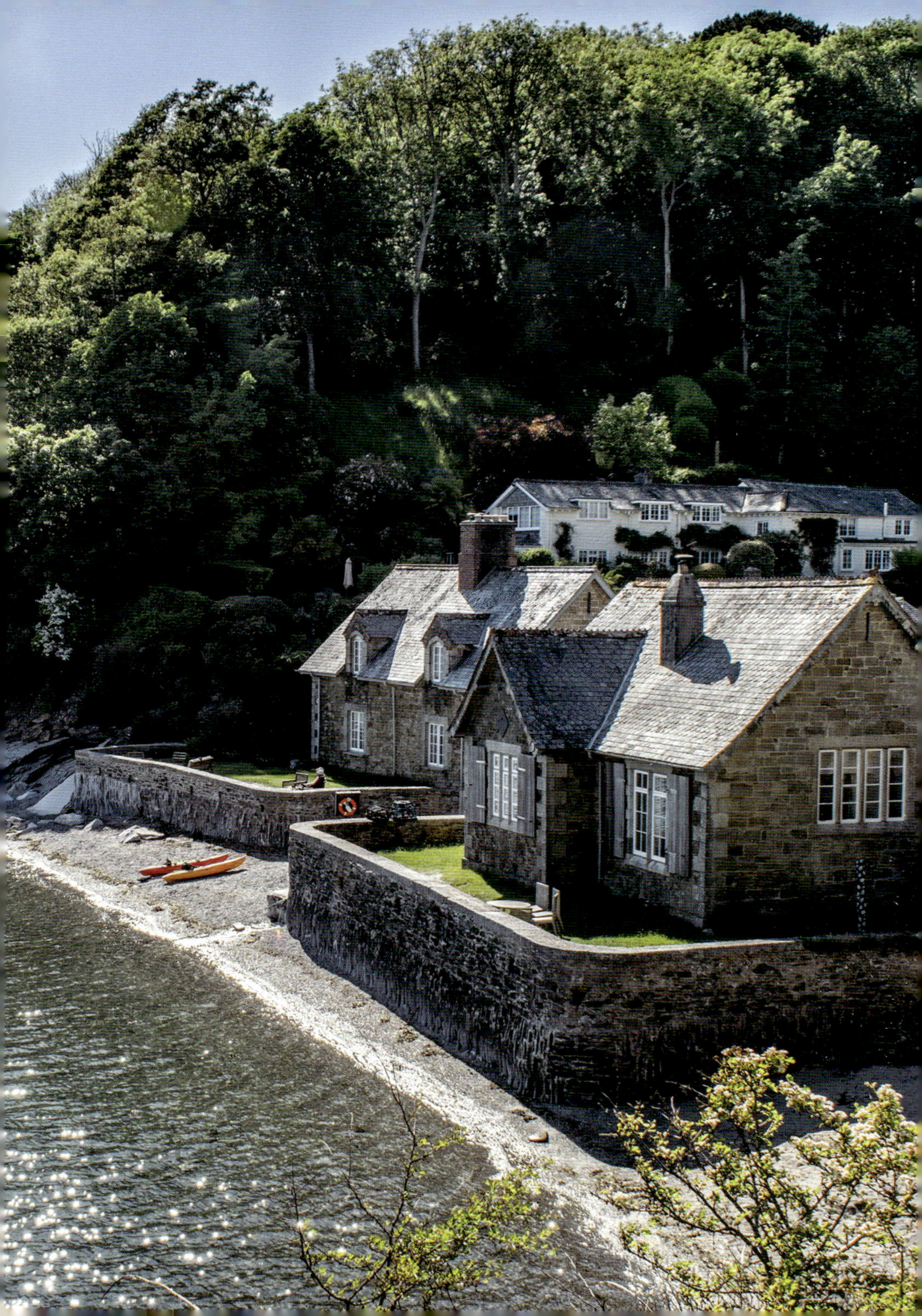

D

name & address **phone**

email

email

email

email

email

email

email

Durgan

D

name & address

phone

email

email

email

email

email

email

email

D

name & address

phone

email

email

email

email

email

email

email

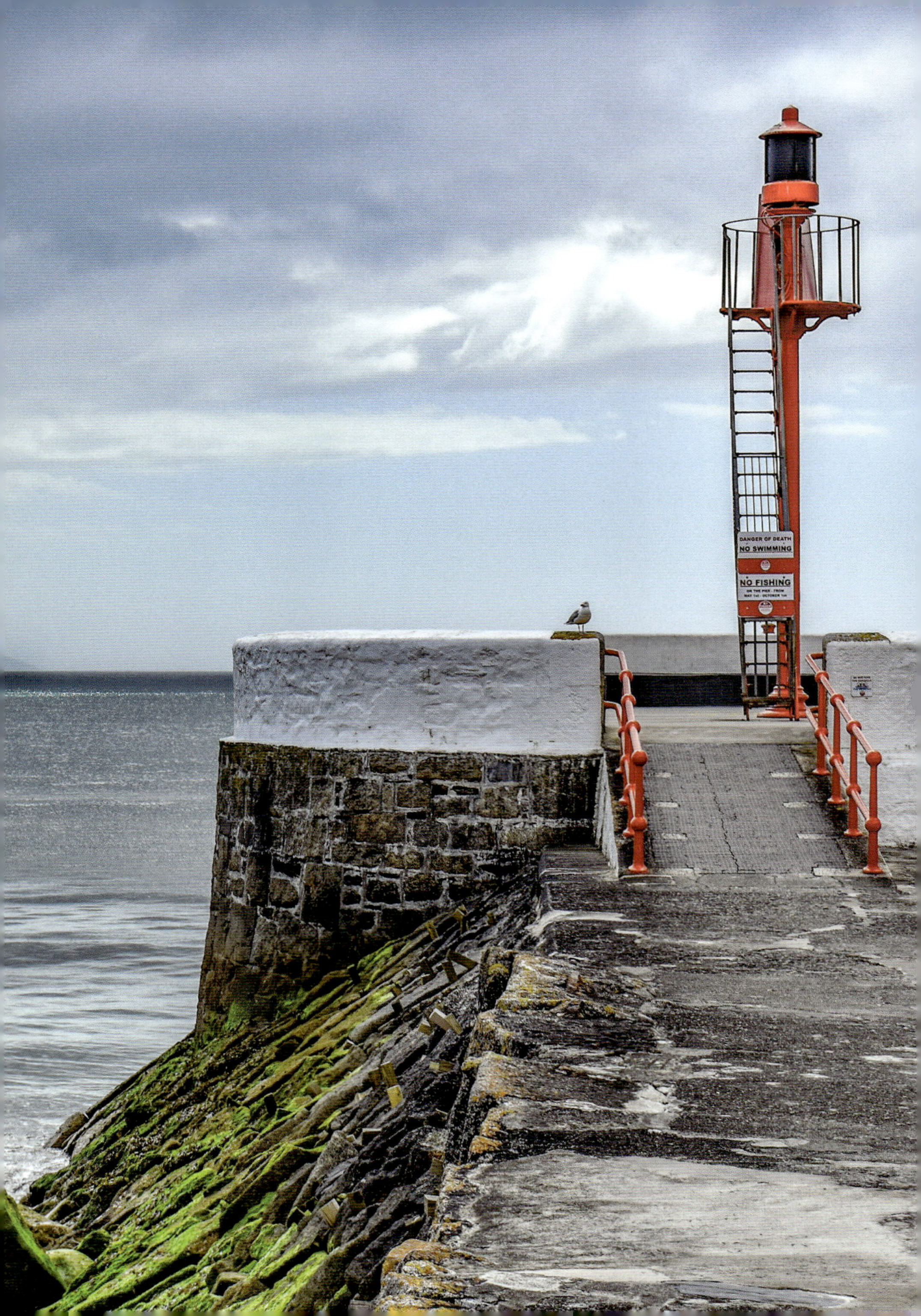
DANGER OF DEATH
NO SWIMMING
NO FISHING

E

name & address　　　　　　　　　　**phone**

email

email

email

email

email

email

email

East Looe

E

name & address **phone**

email

email

email

email

email

email

email

E

name & address **phone**

email

email

email

email

email

email

email

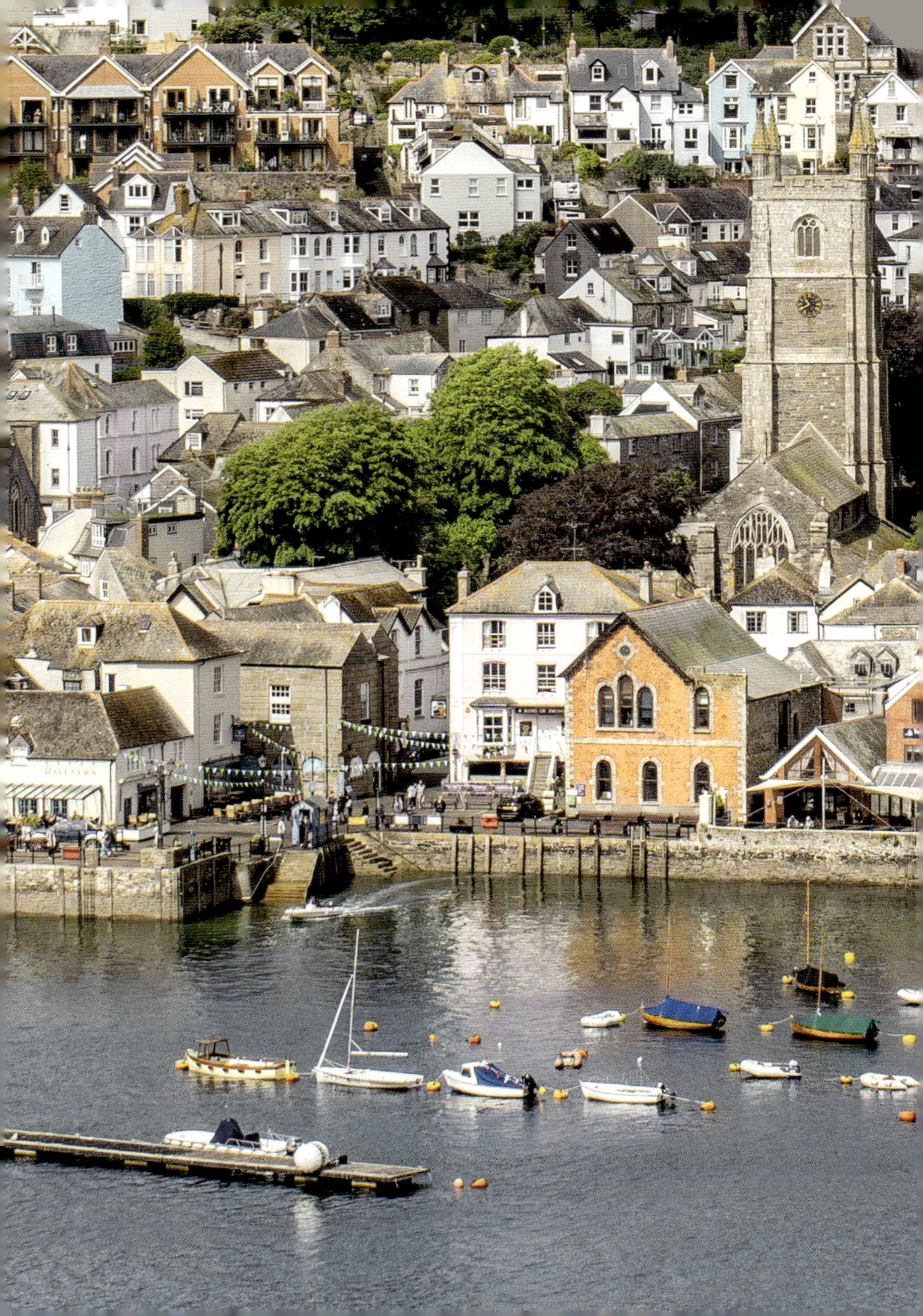
HAVENER'S

F

name & address **phone**

email

email

email

email

email

email

email

Fowey

F

name & address

phone

email

email

email

email

email

email

email

F

name & address

phone

email

email

email

email

email

email

email

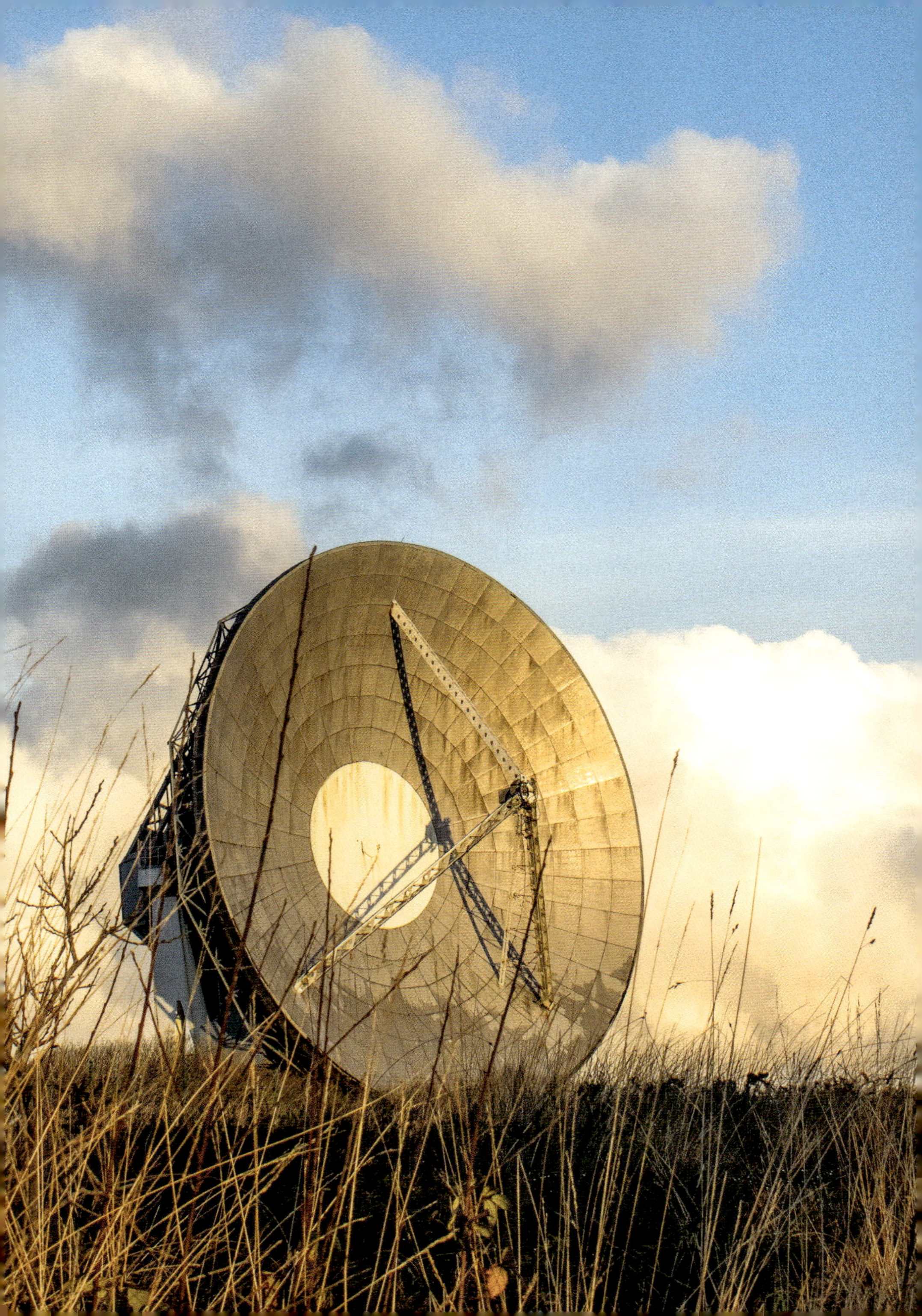

G

name & address **phone**

email

email

email

email

email

email

email

Goonhilly

G

name & address　　　　　　　　　　　　**phone**

email

email

email

email

email

email

email

G

name & address

phone

email

email

email

email

email

email

email

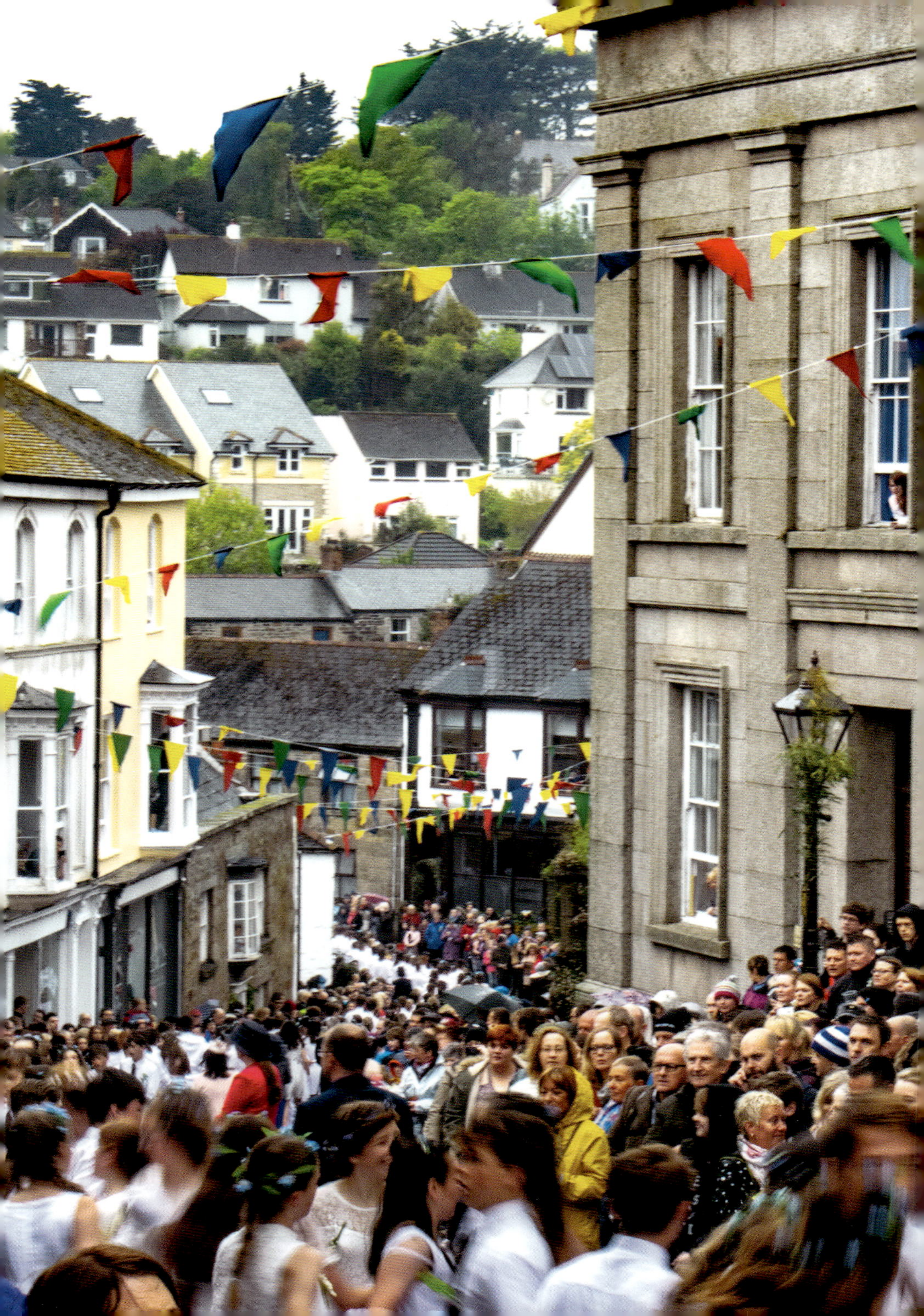

H

name & address phone

email

email

email

email

email

email

email

Helston

H

name & address | **phone**

email

email

email

email

email

email

email

H

name & address

phone

email

email

email

email

email

email

email

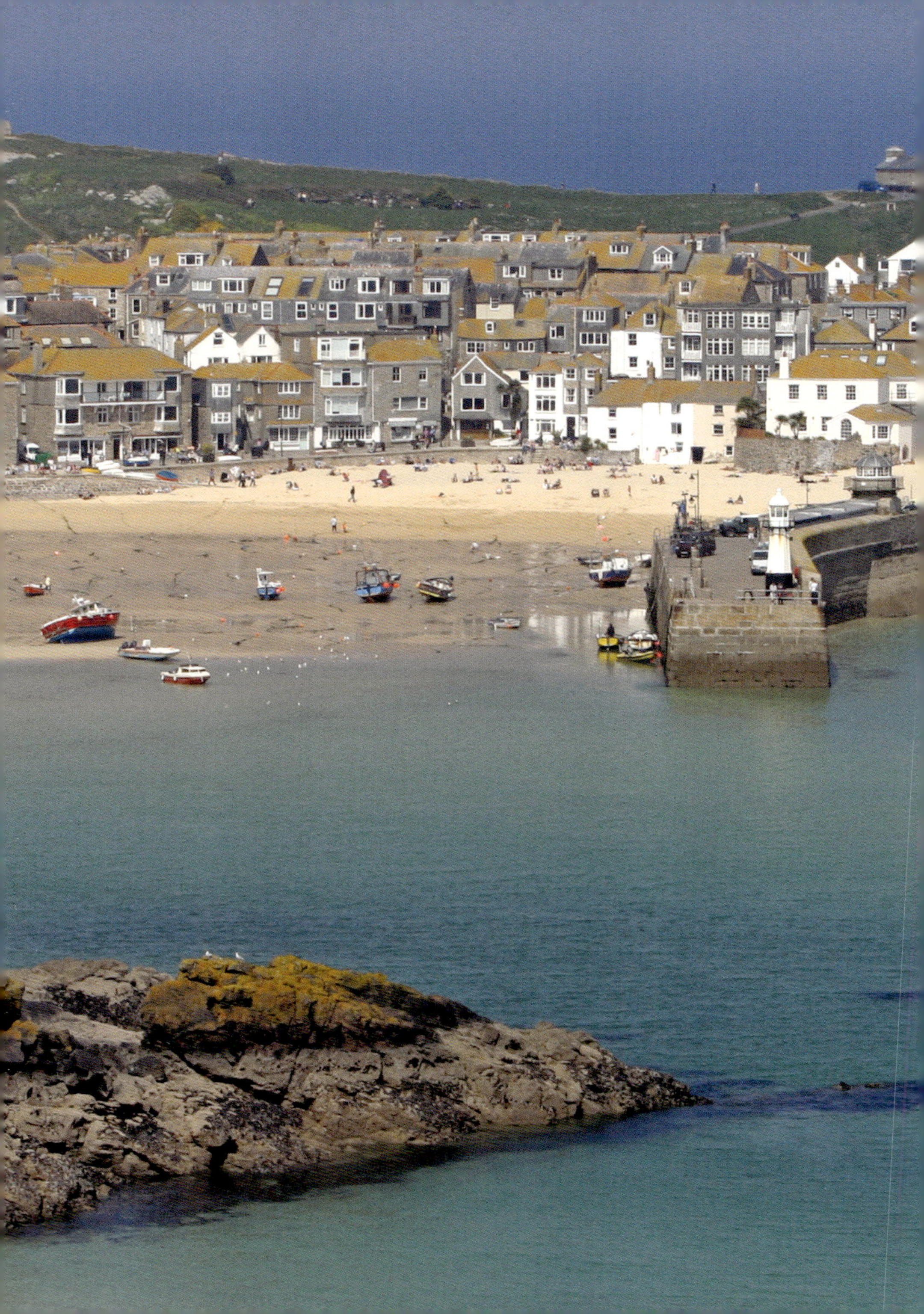

name & address

phone

email

email

email

email

email

email

email

St Ives

name & address

phone

email

email

email

email

email

email

email

name & address

_____
_____

email
_____

_____
_____

email
_____

_____
_____

email
_____

_____
_____

email
_____

_____
_____

email
_____

_____
_____

email
_____

_____
_____

email
_____

phone

_____
_____
_____

_____
_____
_____

_____
_____
_____

_____
_____
_____

_____
_____
_____

_____
_____
_____

_____
_____
_____

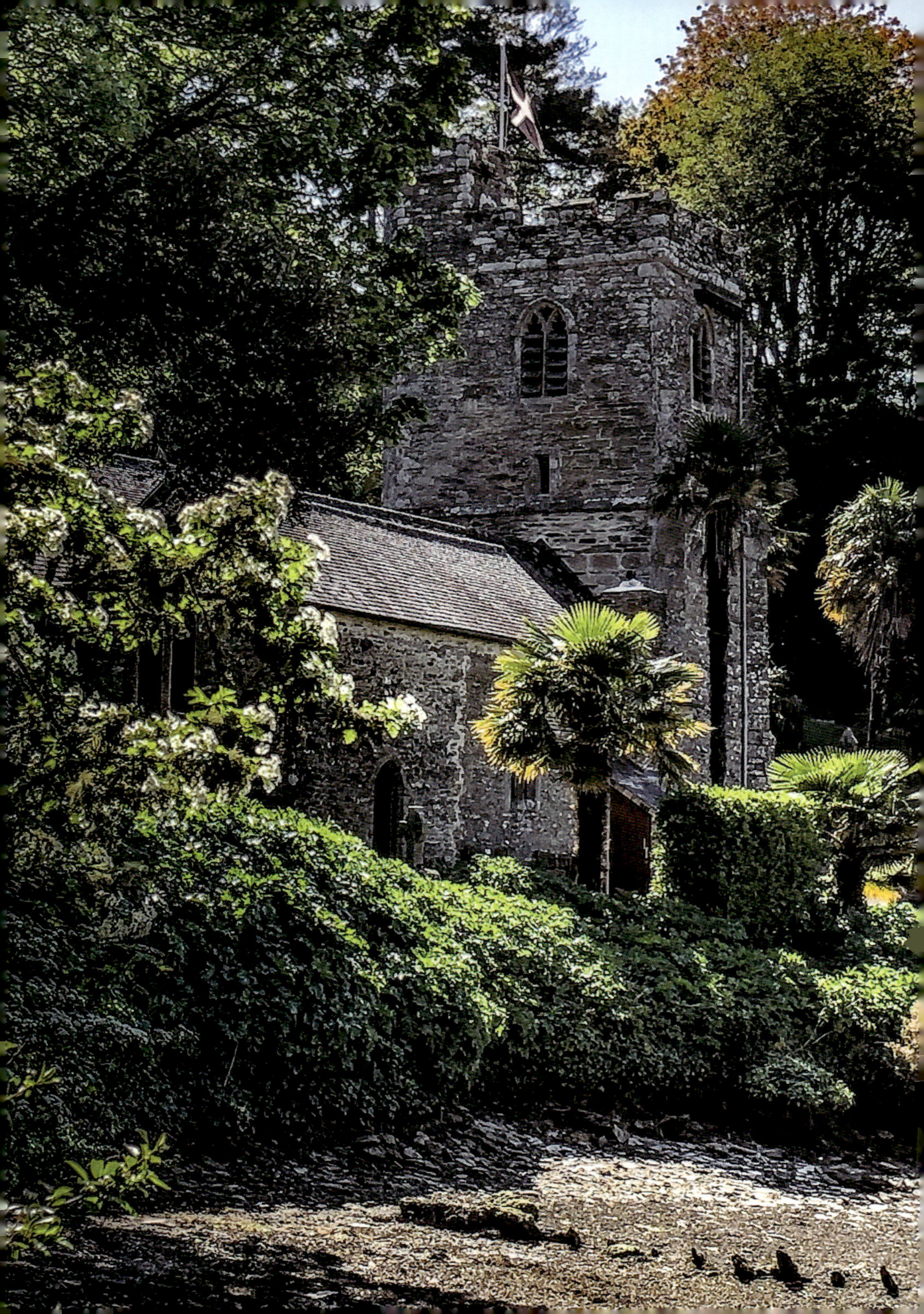

J

name & address **phone**

email

email

email

email

email

email

email

St Just in Roseland

J

name & address   **phone**

email

email

email

email

email

email

email

J

name & address　　　　　　　　　　**phone**

email

email

email

email

email

email

email

email

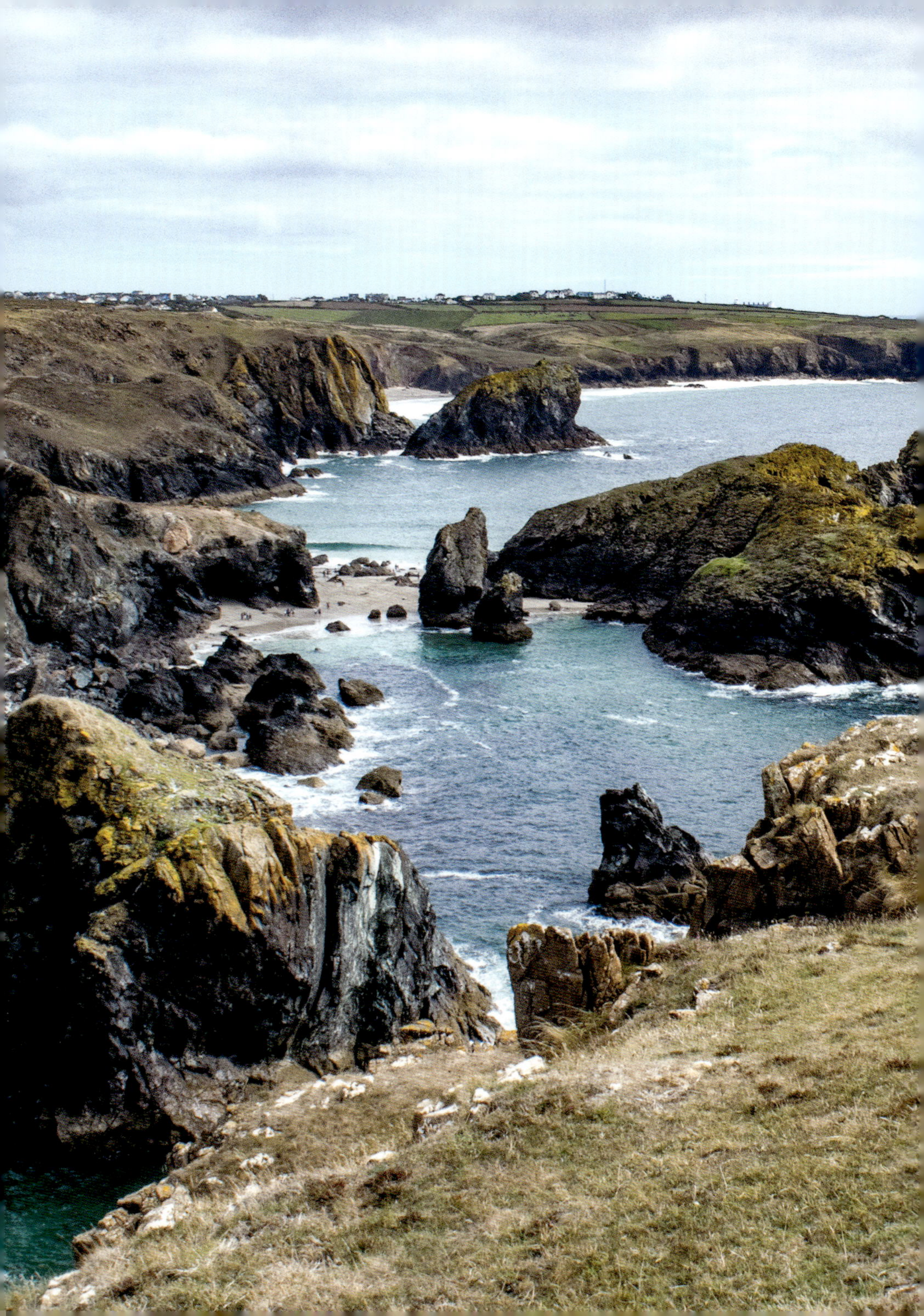

K

name & address

phone

email

email

email

email

email

email

email

Kynance

K

name & address

phone

email

email

email

email

email

email

email

K

name & address

phone

email

email

email

email

email

email

email

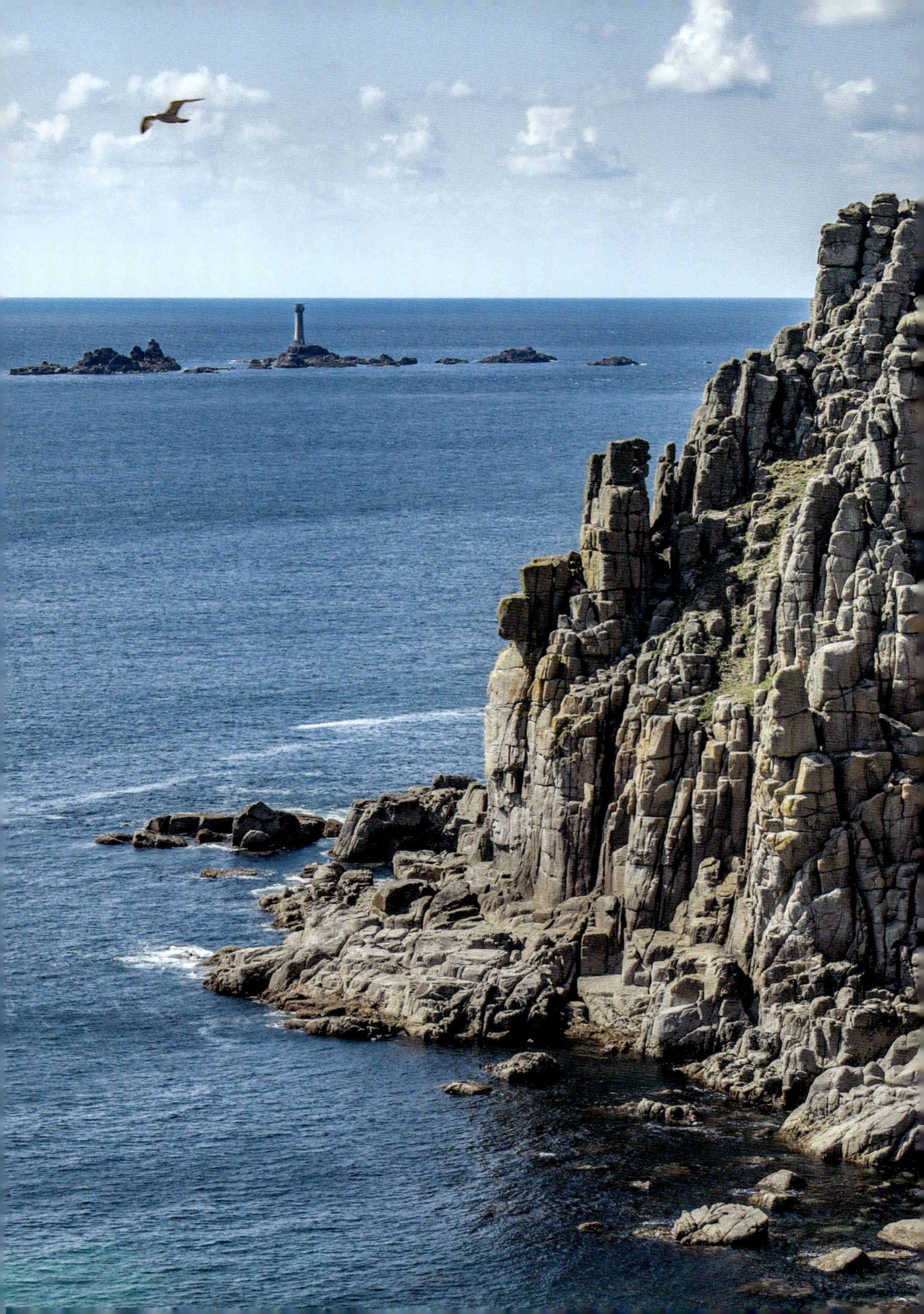

L

name & address **phone**

email

email

email

email

email

email

email

Land's End

L

name & address **phone**

email

email

email

email

email

email

email

L

name & address phone

email

email

email

email

email

email

email

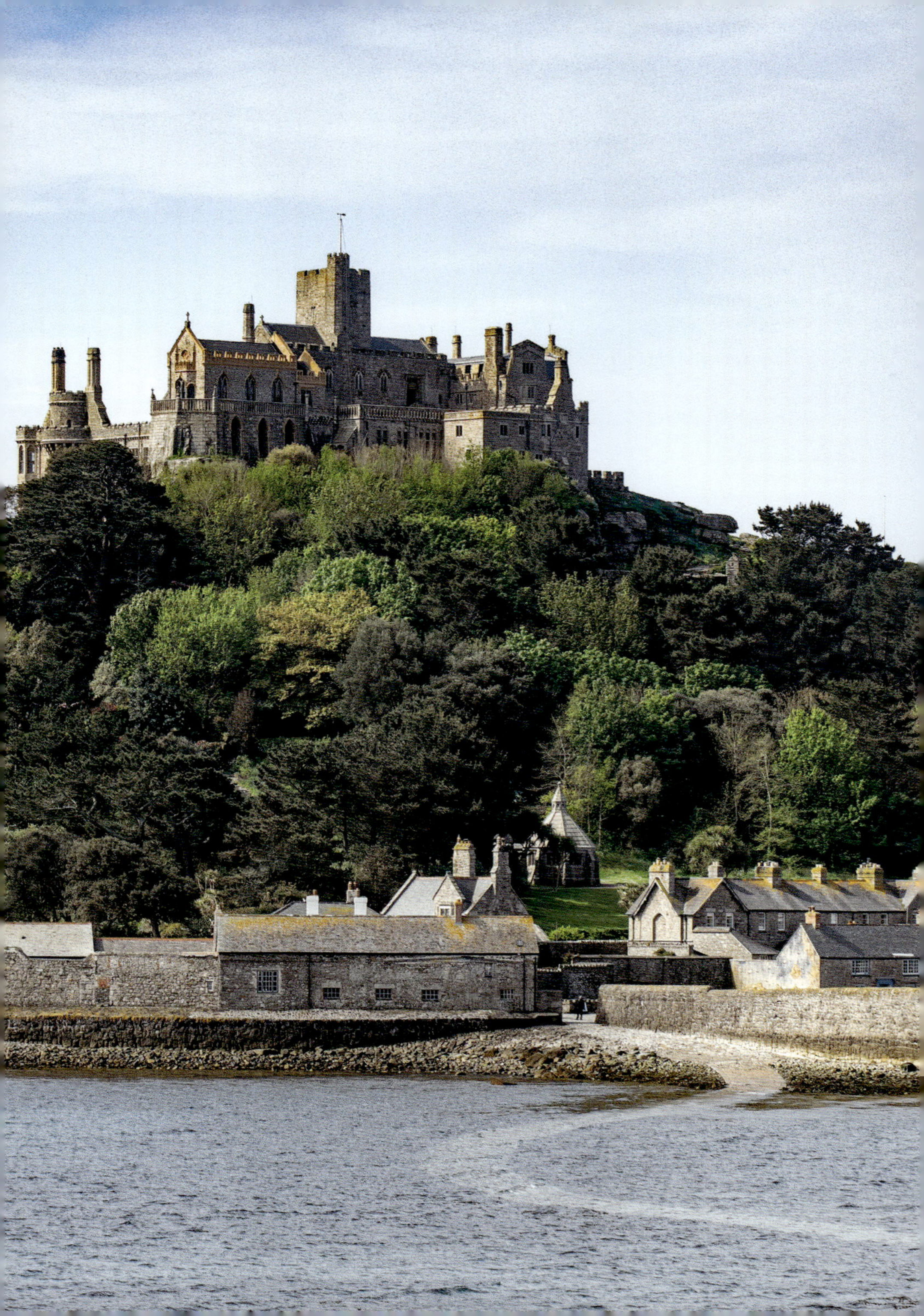

M

name & address | **phone**

email

email

email

email

email

email

email

St Michael's Mount

M

name & address **phone**

email

email

email

email

email

email

email

M

name & address | **phone**

email

email

email

email

email

email

email

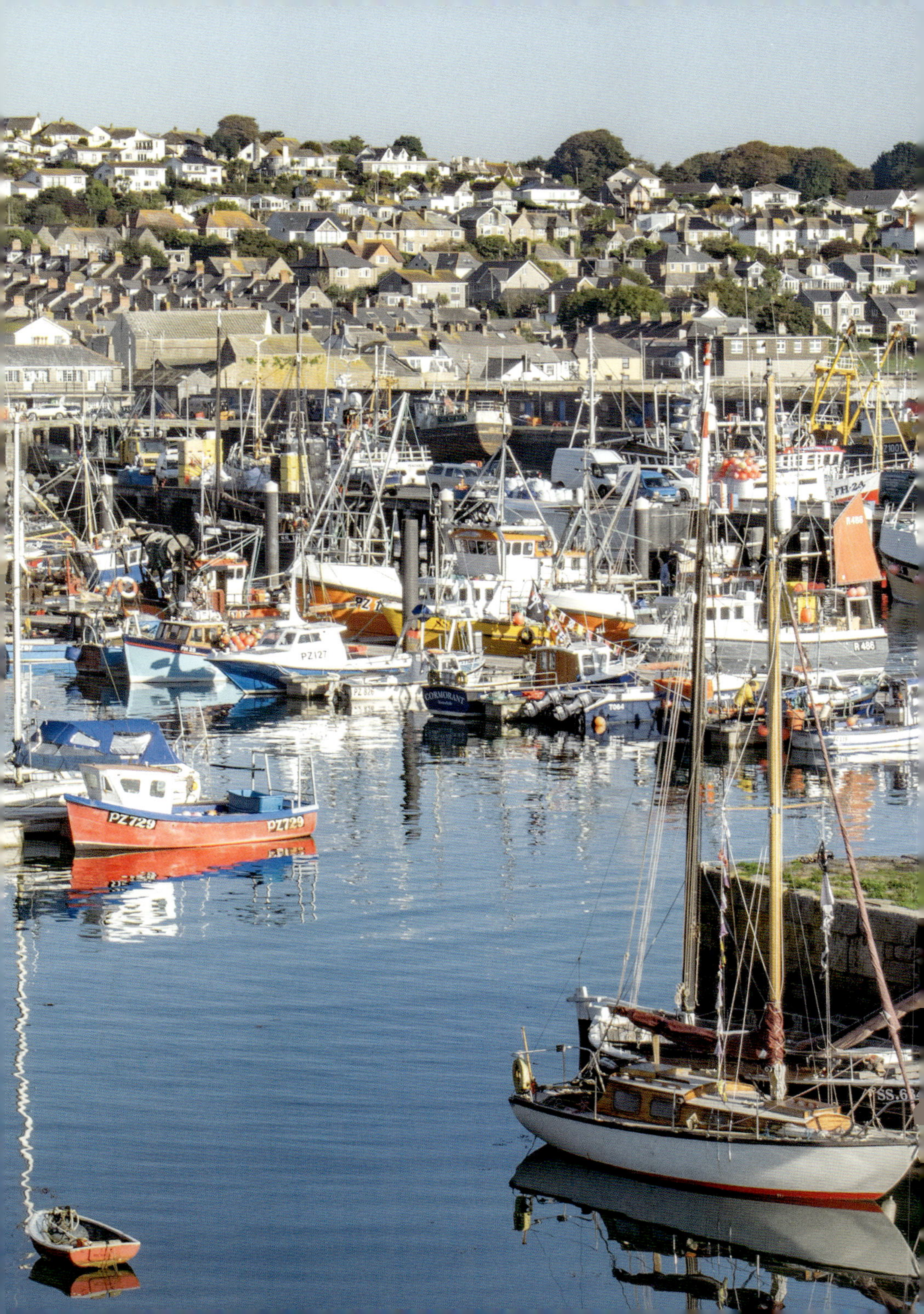
PZ729
PZ729
PZ127
R 486
CORMORANT

N

name & address **phone**

email

email

email

email

email

email

email

Newlyn

N

name & address   **phone**

email

email

email

email

email

email

email

N

name & address

phone

email

email

email

email

email

email

email

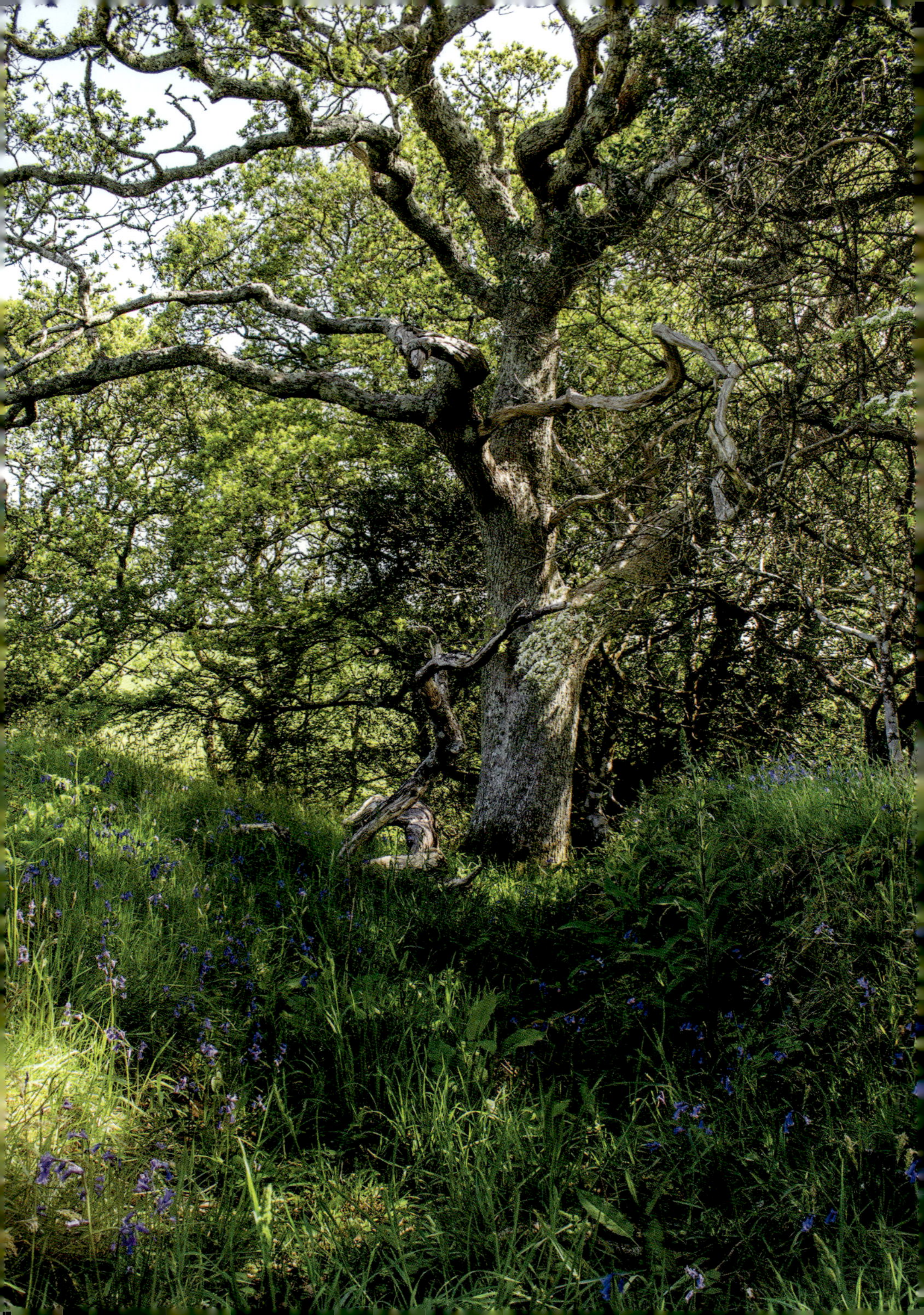

O

name & address **phone**

email

email

email

email

email

email

email

Old Cardinham

name & address

phone

email

email

email

email

email

email

email

O

name & address

phone

email

email

email

email

email

email

email

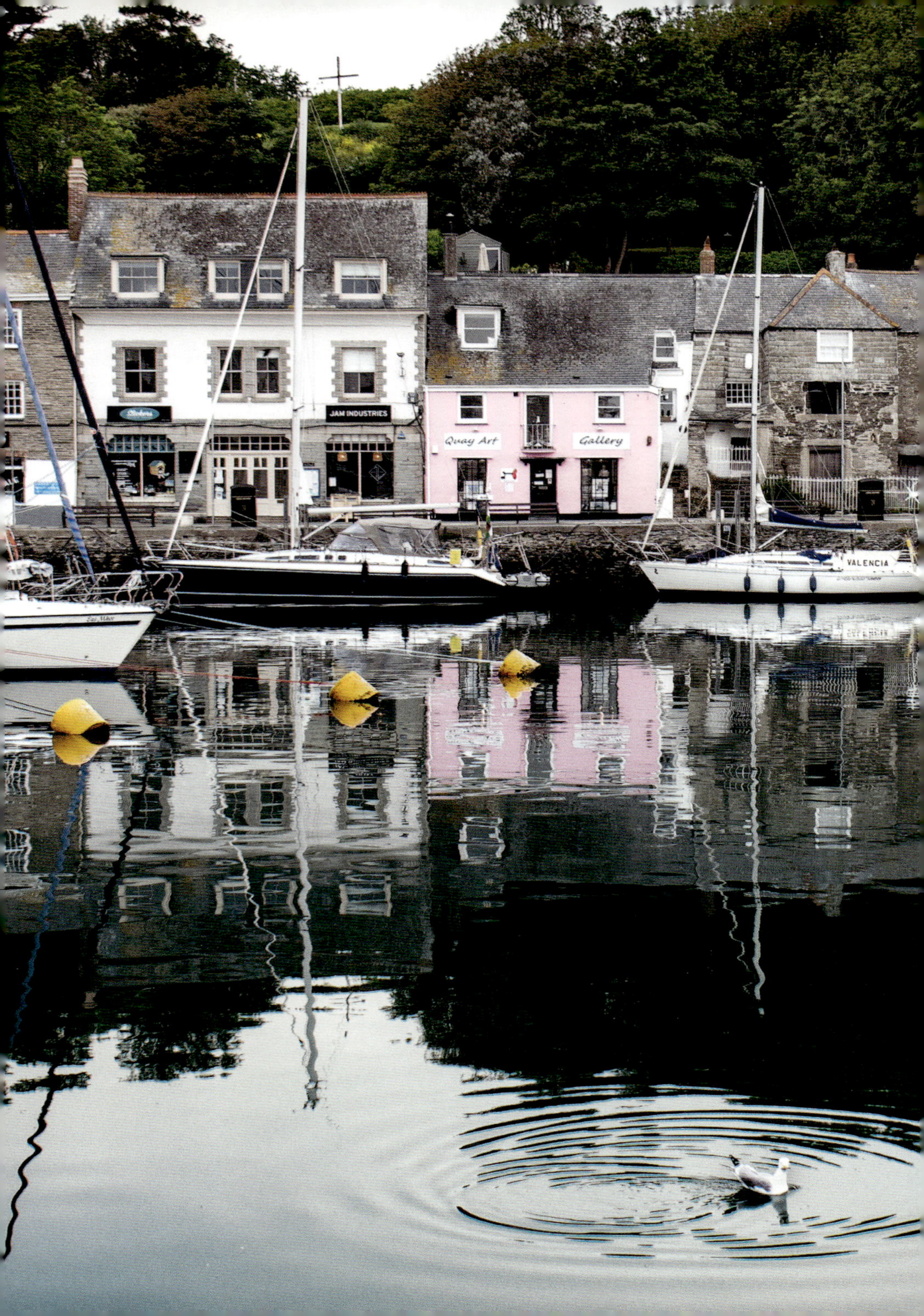
JAM INDUSTRIES
Quay Art
Gallery
VALENCIA

P

name & address

phone

email

email

email

email

email

email

email

Padstow

P

name & address | **phone**

email

email

email

email

email

email

email

P

name & address | **phone**

email

email

email

email

email

email

email

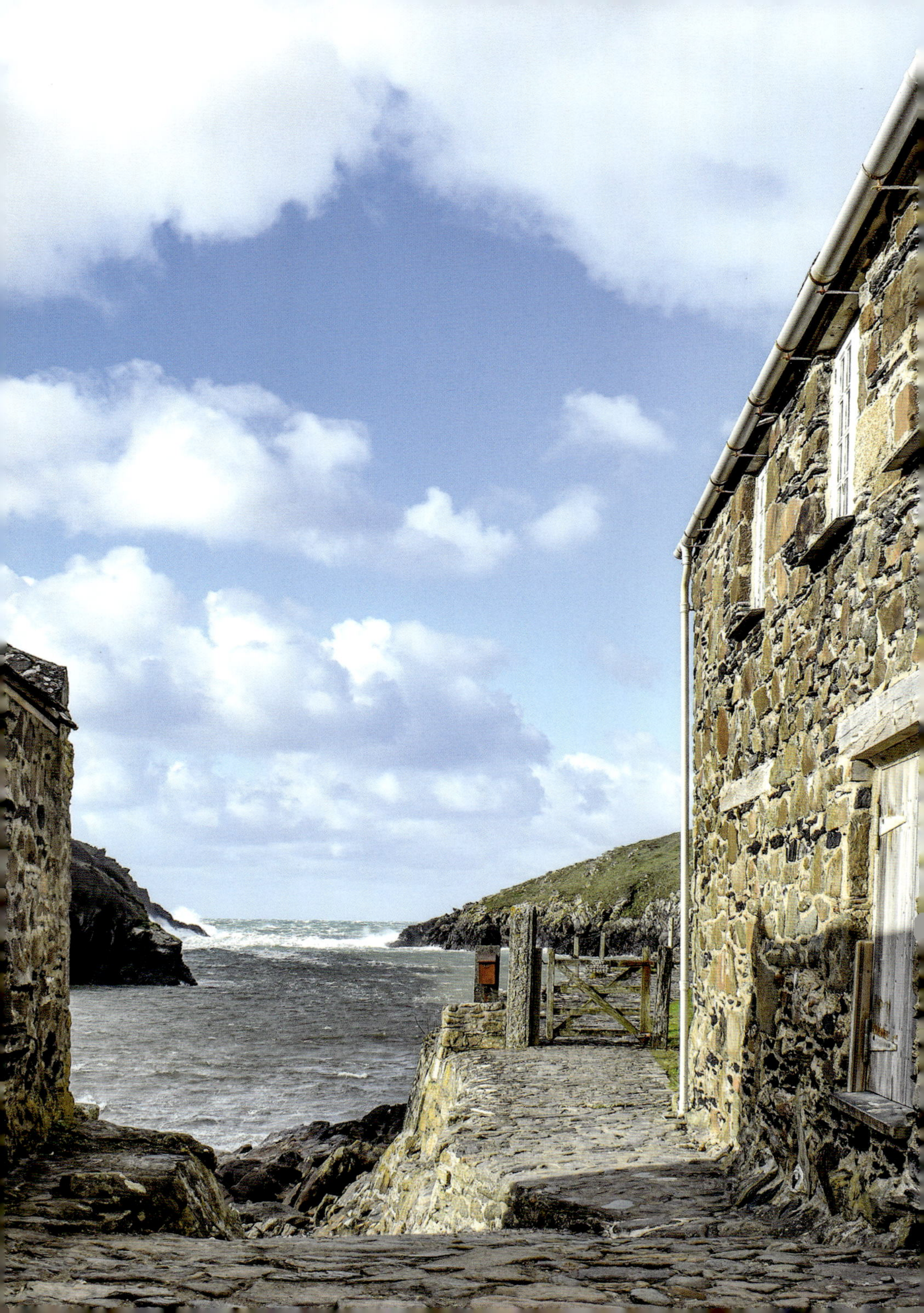

Q

name & address　　　　　　　　　　**phone**

email

email

email

email

email

email

email

Port Quin

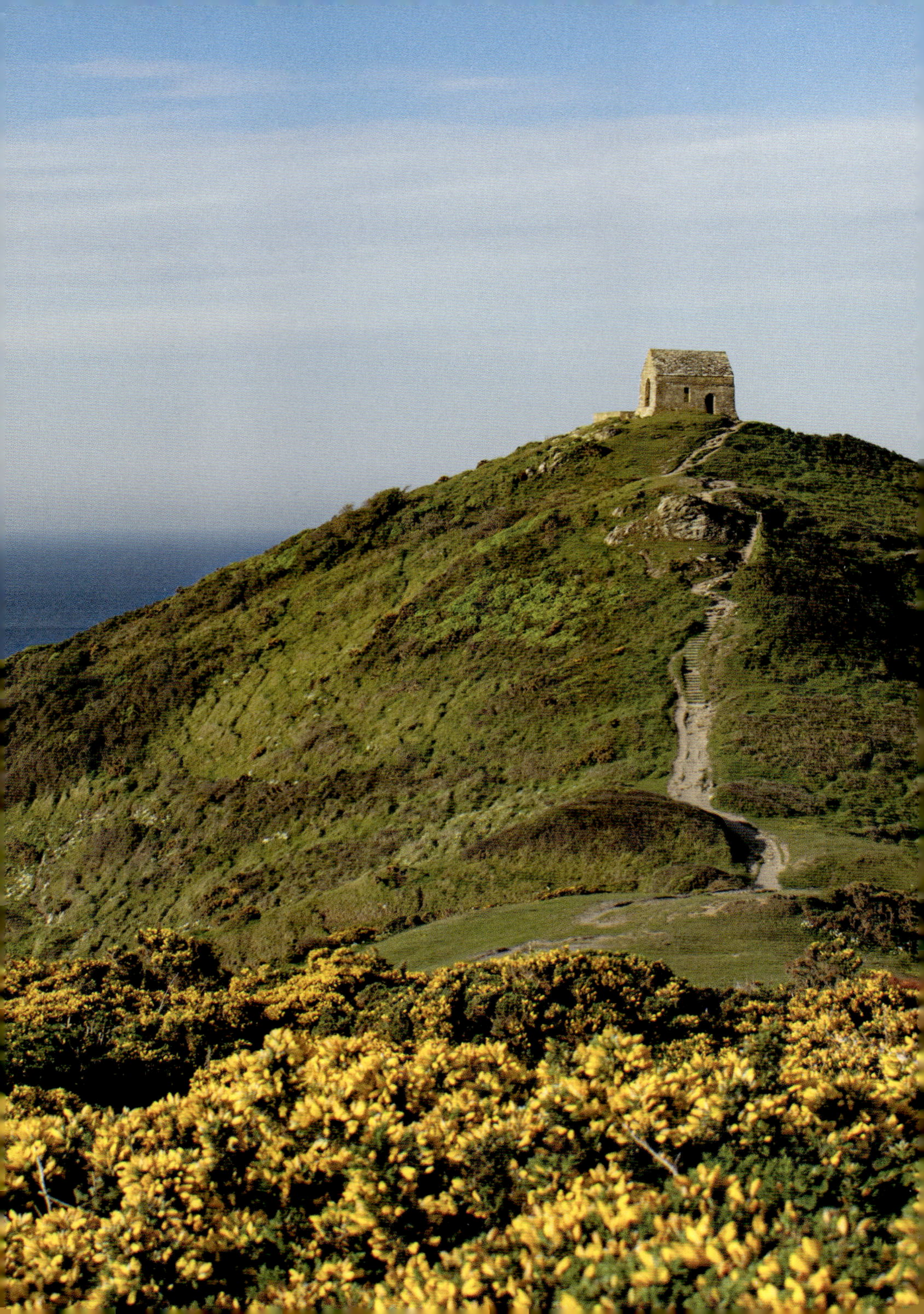

R

name & address **phone**

email

email

email

email

email

email

email

Rame Head

R

name & address

phone

email

email

email

email

email

email

email

R

name & address

phone

email

email

email

email

email

email

email

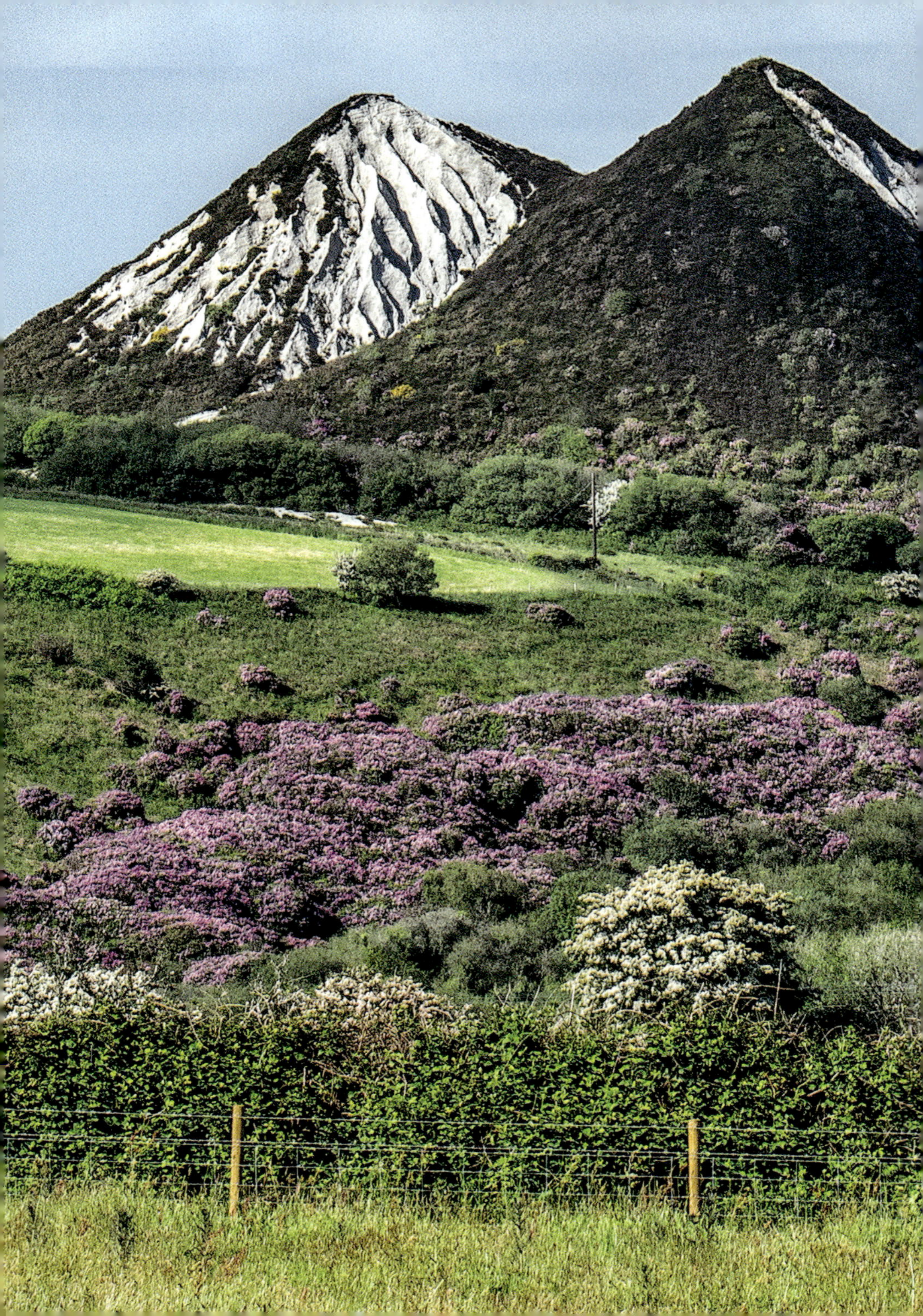

S

name & address　　　　　　　　　　**phone**

email

email

email

email

email

email

email

St Austell

S

name & address **phone**

email

email

email

email

email

email

email

S

name & address **phone**

email

email

email

email

email

email

email

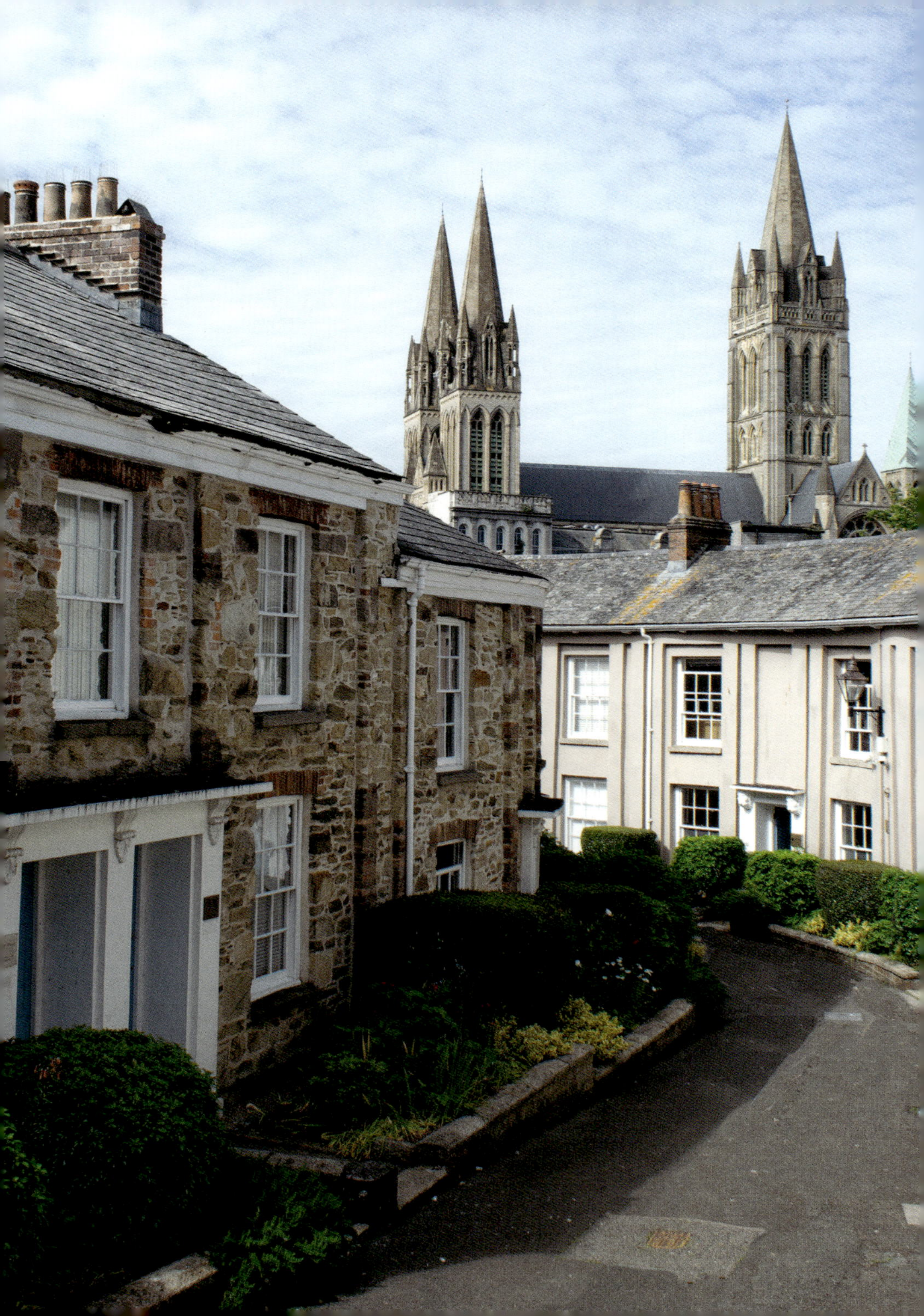

T

name & address

phone

email

email

email

email

email

email

email

Truro

T

name & address **phone**

email

email

email

email

email

email

email

T

name & address

phone

email

email

email

email

email

email

email

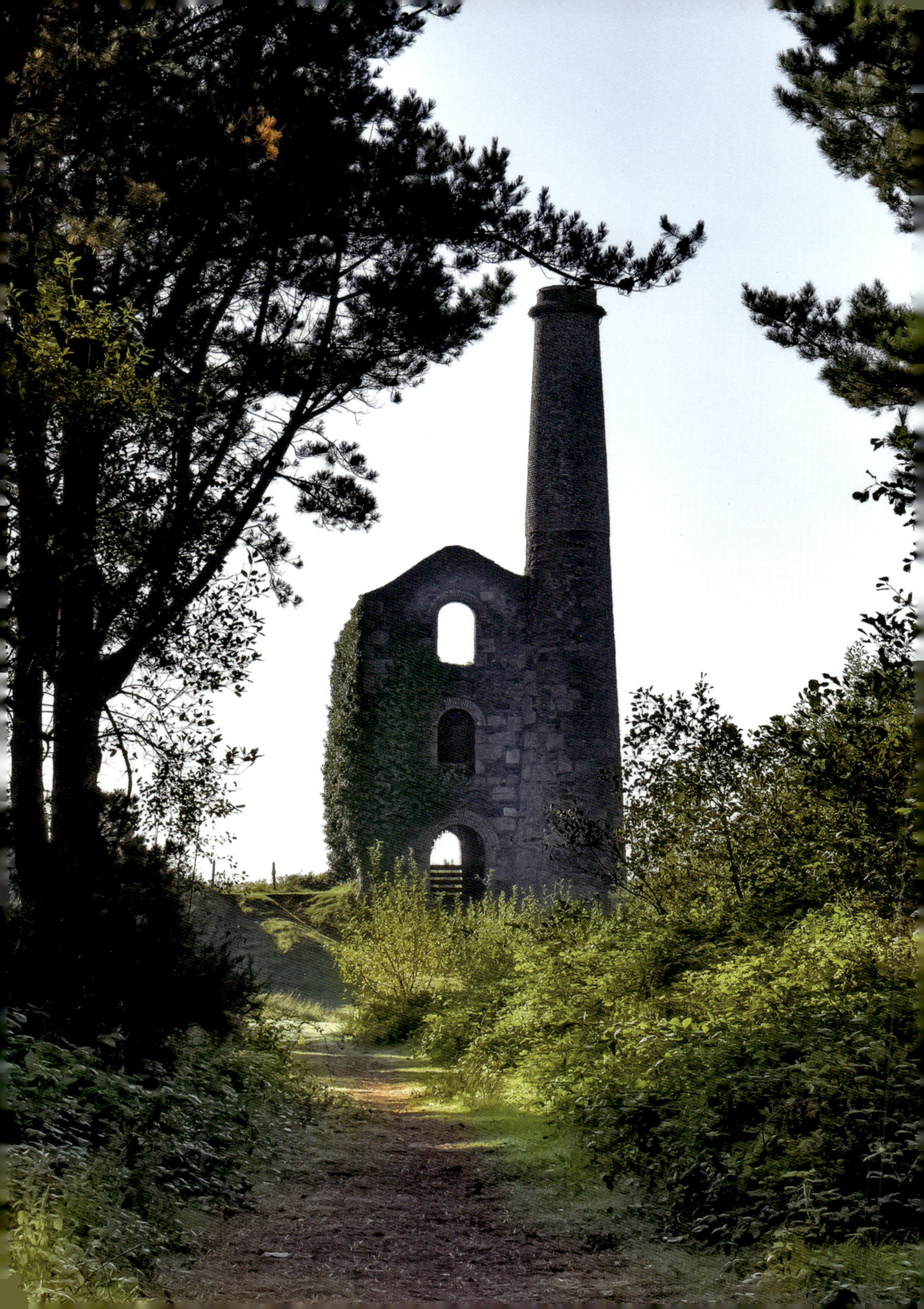

U

name & address

phone

email

email

email

email

email

email

email

United Downs

U

name & address

phone

email

email

email

email

email

email

email

U

name & address **phone**

email

email

email

email

email

email

email

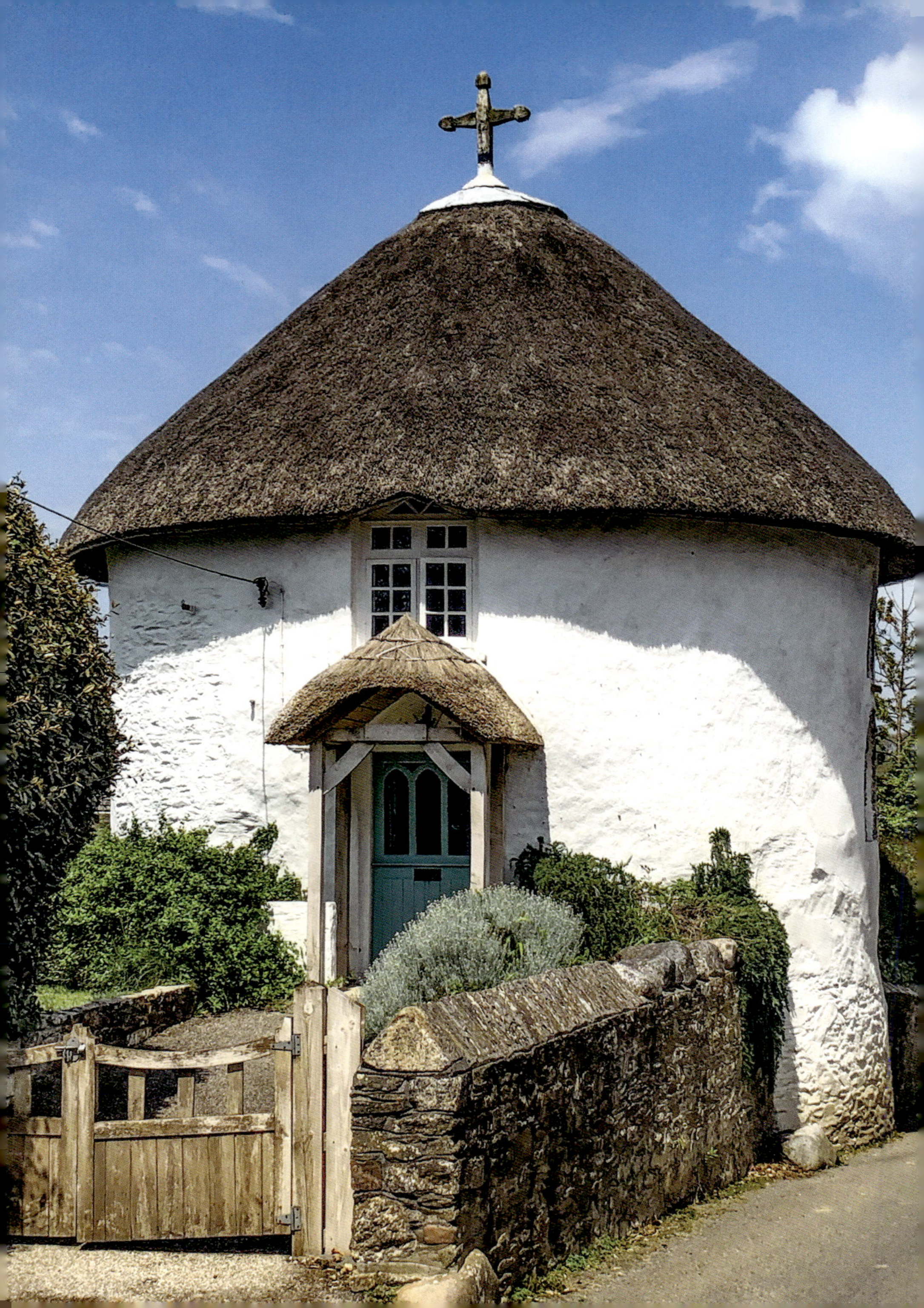

V

name & address **phone**

email

email

email

email

email

email

email

Veryan

V

name & address　　　　　　　　　　　**phone**

email

email

email

email

email

email

email

V

name & address phone

email

email

email

email

email

email

email

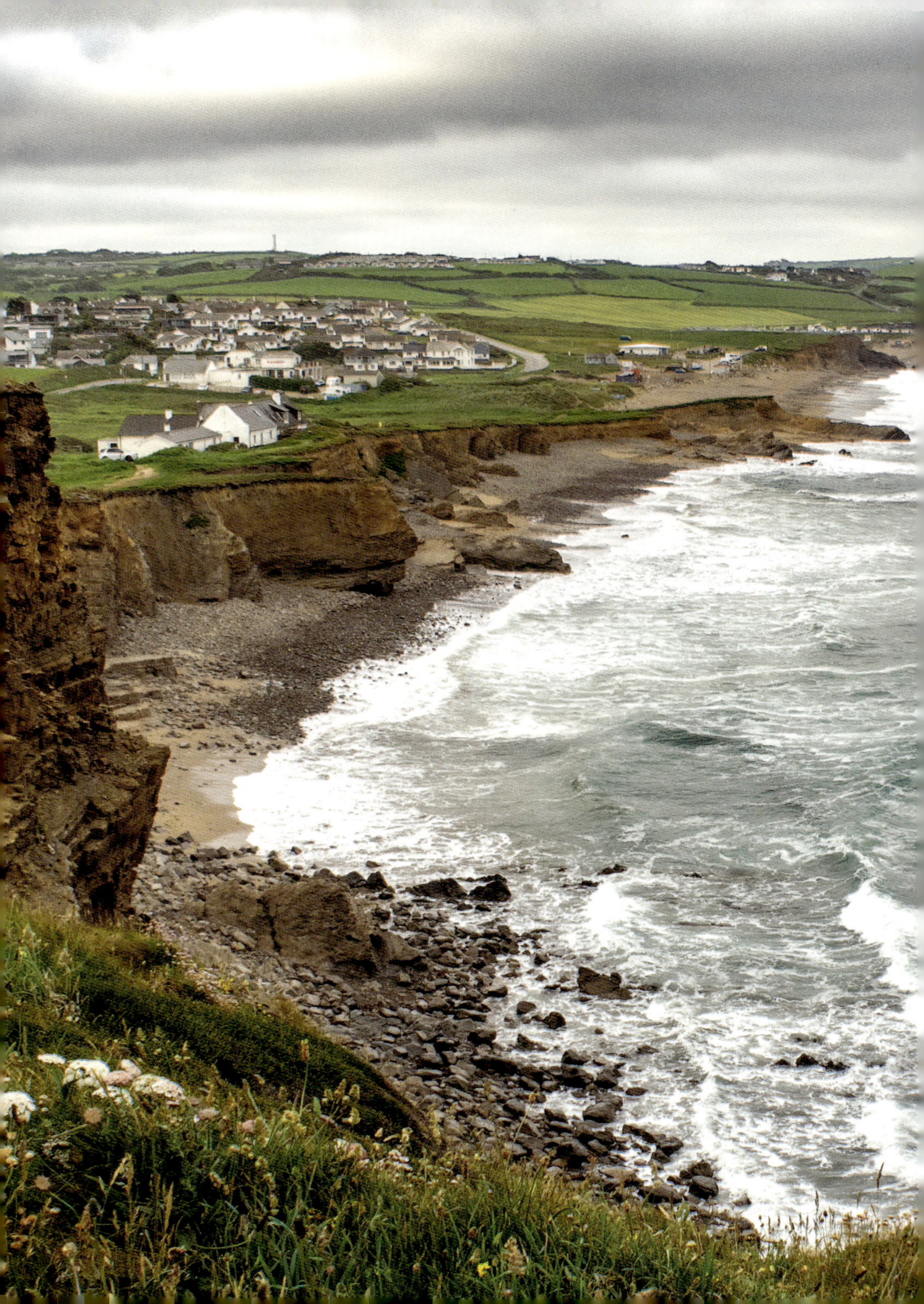

W

name & address phone

email

email

email

email

email

email

email

Widemouth Bay

W

name & address   **phone**

email

email

email

email

email

email

email

W

name & address **phone**

email

email

email

email

email

email

email

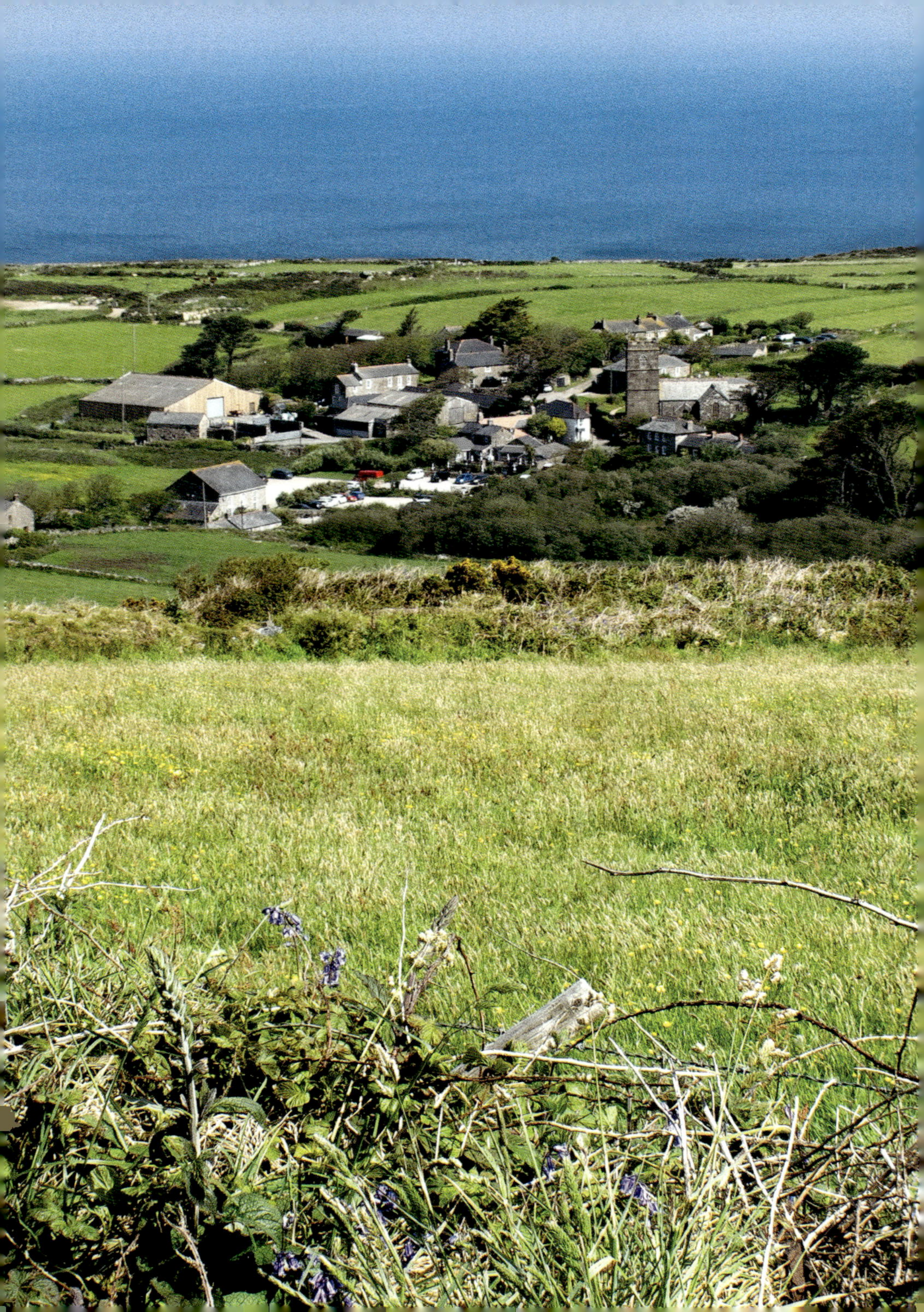

XYZ

name & address **phone**

email

email

email

email

email

email

email

Zennor

XYZ

name & address **phone**

email

email

email

email

email

email

email

XYZ

name & address

phone

email

email

email

email

email

email

email

January

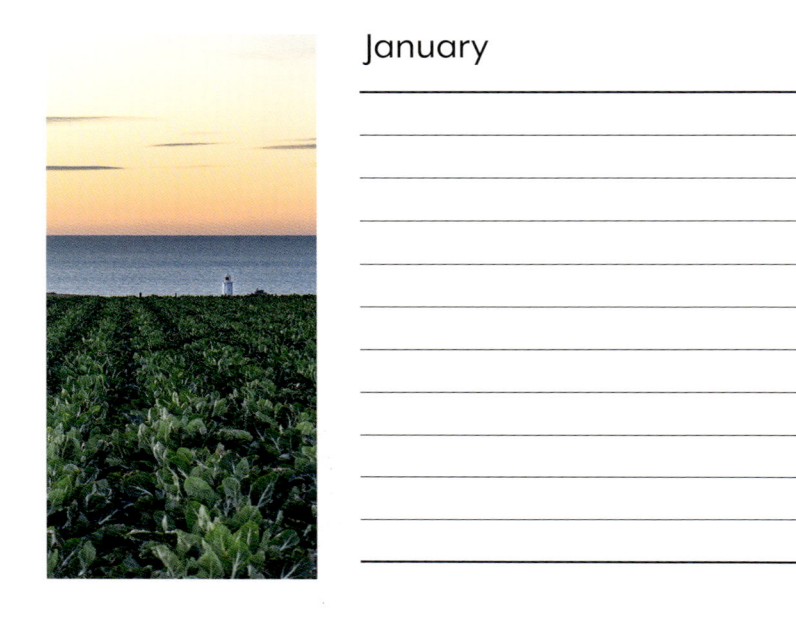

February

March

April

May

June

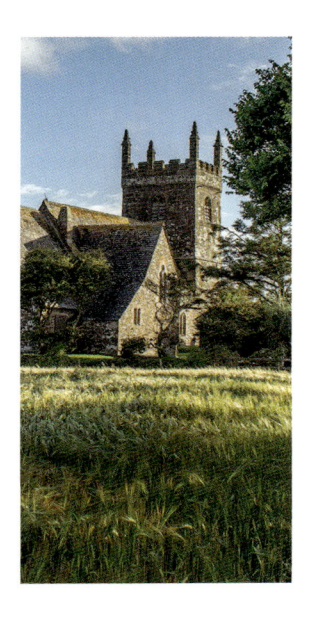

July

August

September

October

Useful to remember

November

December

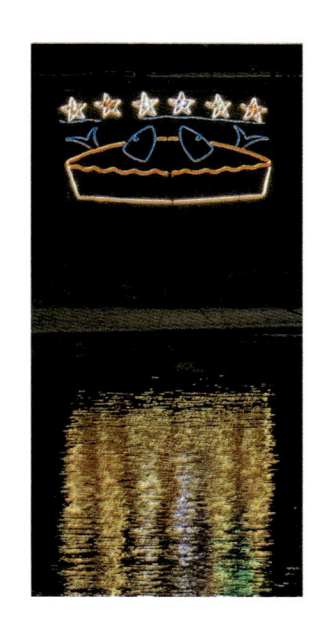